Leaping Lizards

MathStart®
COUNTING BY 5s AND 10s

Leaping Lizards

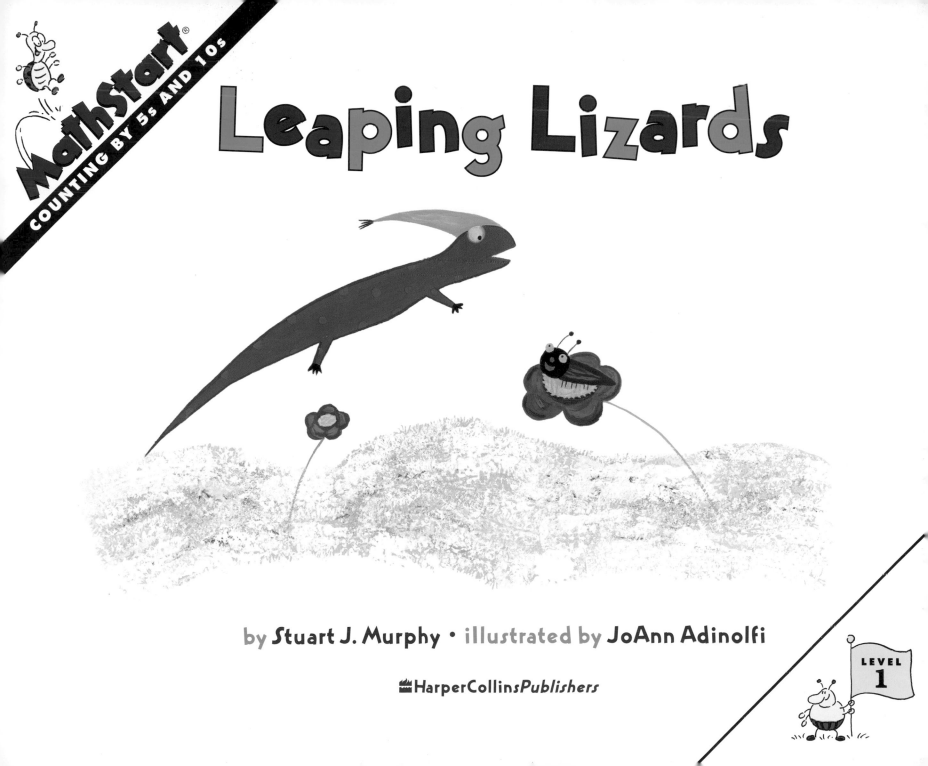

by **Stuart J. Murphy** • illustrated by **JoAnn Adinolfi**

HarperCollinsPublishers

LEVEL
1

To Camilla, who leaps like a lizard
—S.J.M.

To Karsten, my mathematical lizard
—J.A.

The publisher and author would like to thank teachers
Patricia Chase, Phyllis Goldman, and Patrick Hopfensperger
for their help in making the math in MathStart just right for kids.

HarperCollins®, ☕ ®, and MathStart® are registered trademarks of HarperCollins Publishers.
For more information about the MathStart series, write to
HarperCollins Children's Books, 1350 Avenue of the Americas, New York, NY 10019

Bugs incorporated in the MathStart series design were painted by Jon Buller.

Leaping Lizards

ISBN 0-06-000132-1

Typography by Elynn Cohen

Be sure to look for all of these **MathStart** books:

Lazy lizards—
time to go!
Let's get ready
for the show.

One, two, three, four,
five of you.
Not enough!
What will we do?

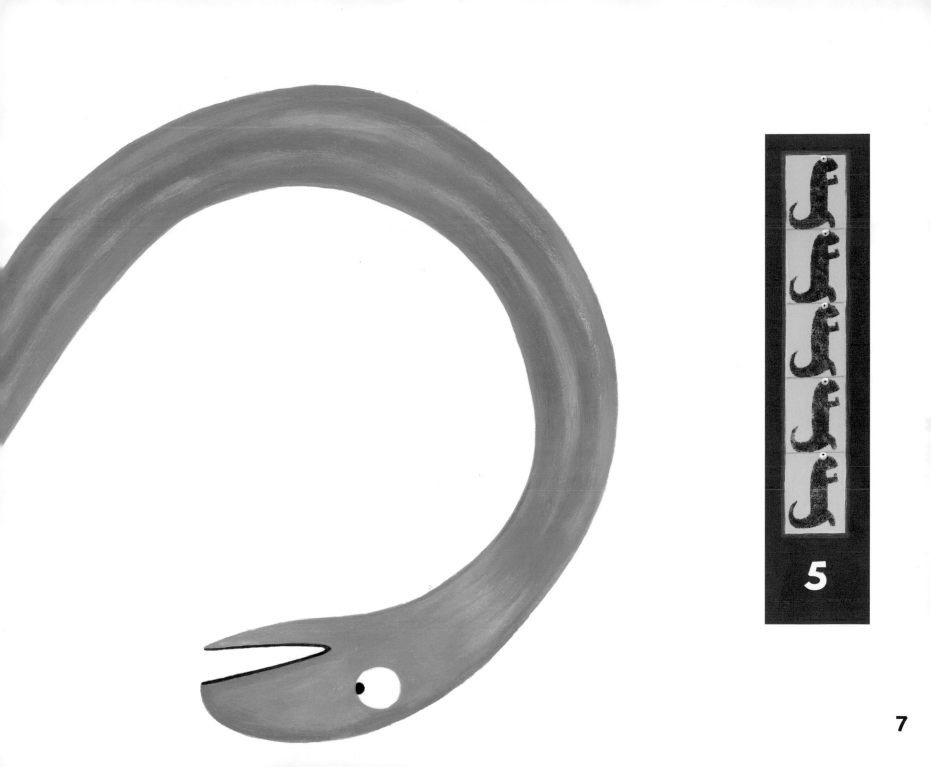

We need fifty
to take part,
or this show
can never start.

Look! Five more
come riding in.
Add them up!
Now there are ten.

5   10

Five rush up
in racing cars.
I can count
fifteen so far.

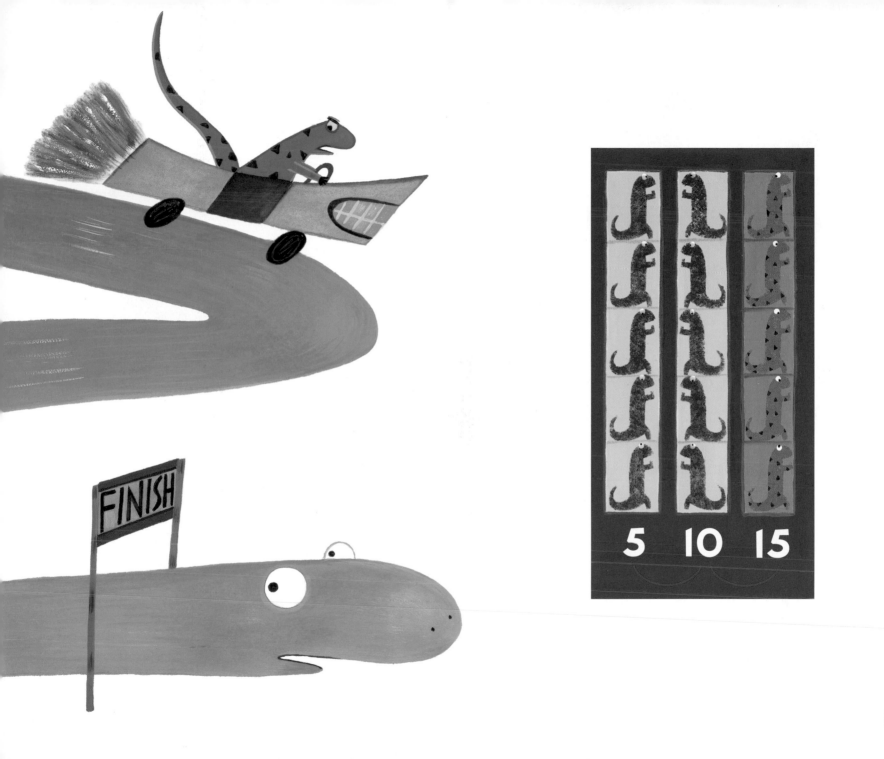

FINISH

5   10   15

13

Five fly by
in a balloon.
That's twenty if they
come down soon!

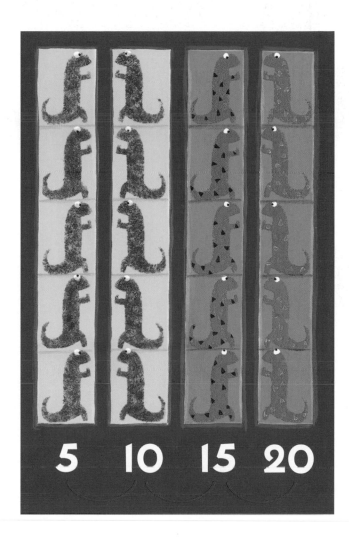

5   10   15   20

Five swim up.
When they arrive,
that's half of fifty—
twenty-five.

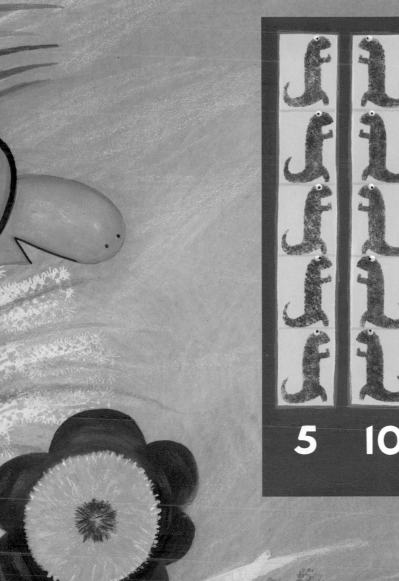

5 10 15 20 25

18

I lost count!
Let's start again.
The first two fives
can make a ten.

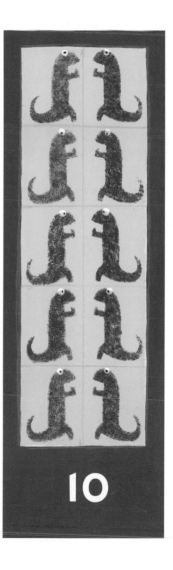

10

Two more fives
make ten more—great!
Twenty now.
We can't be late.

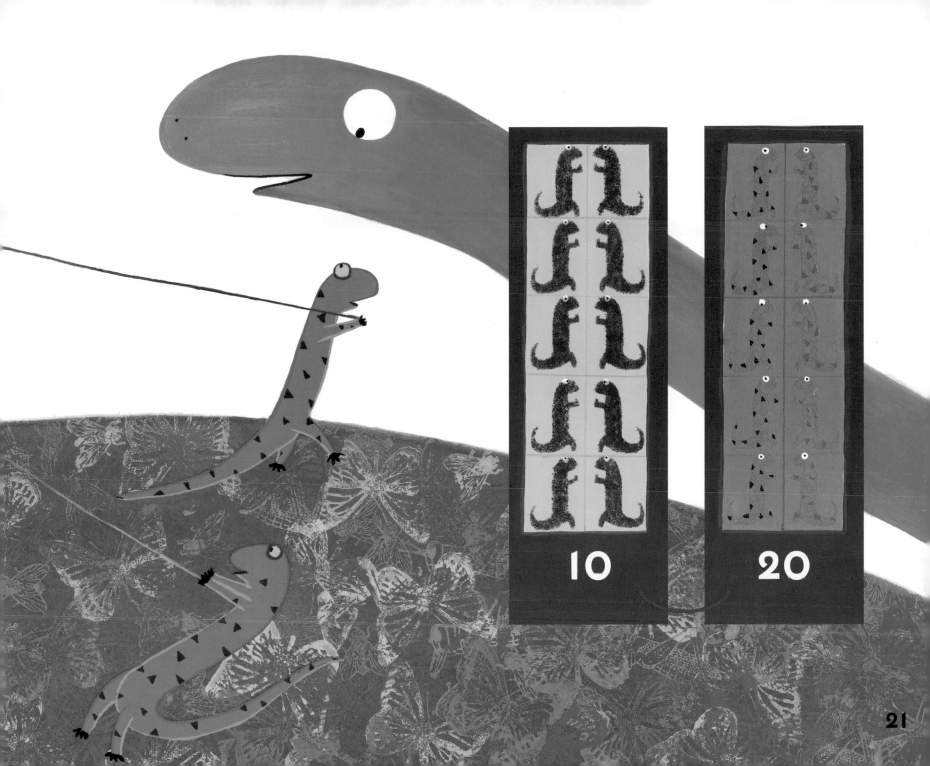

10   20

21

Five who swam—that's
twenty-five.
Now look who's coming
up the drive.

Five new lizards
in their trucks.
Thirty lizards!
We're in luck!

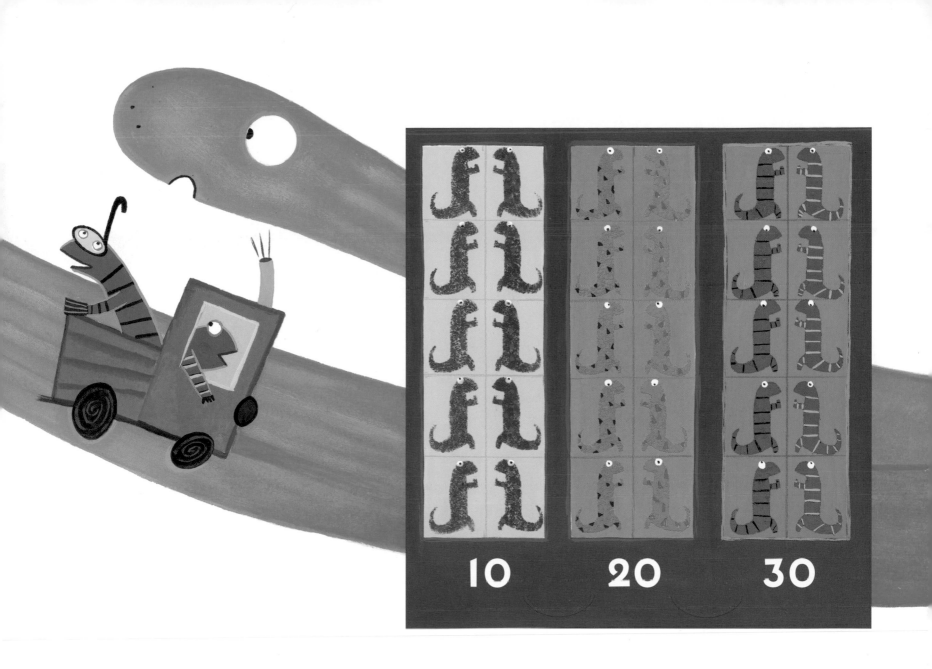

10   20   30

23

Ten sail up
in fine, clear weather.
Forty lizards
altogether.

10　　20　　30　　40

Ten touch down
in one huge jet.
Fifty lizards—
we're all set!

10   20   30   40   50

Flies and skeeters:
What's in store?
This is what
you've waited for.

Are you ready?
Set? Let's go—

The Fifty Leaping Lizards Show!

n *Leaping Lizards*, the math concept is counting by fives and tens. This skill helps children learn to count money, tell time, and master multiplication facts.

If you would like to have more fun with the math concepts presented in *Leaping Lizards*, here are a few suggestions:

- Read the story with the child and count the number of lizards in each picture. Remind the child that you are trying to reach a goal of 50.

- Reread the story together with small objects at hand, such as pennies or buttons. Encourage the child to use the objects to act out the story. Help the child see how two groups of 5 are combined to form a group of 10.

- Gather 50 playing blocks and have the child make groups of 5. Then put the groups of 5 together in pairs to make groups of 10.

- Using a calculator, help the child enter the digit 5. Then add 5 and note the sum. Continue adding 5 until you reach 50, noting the sum each time. Note that adding 5 each time is the same as counting by 5s. Repeat by 10s.

- Have the child find out how many fingers and toes are in the family. Encourage the child to count by 5s and 10s.

Following are some activities that will help you extend the concepts presented in *Leaping Lizards* into a child's everyday life:

5s and 10s Game: You will need two decks of playing cards. Remove the face cards and the aces. Shuffle the remaining cards. The players take turns turning over a card. If a card is a 5 or 10, the player keeps it. The first person whose cards total 50 wins.

Clock Work: Show the child a clock with hands. Explain how each number on the face of the clock indicates 5 minutes. Have the child count the groups of 5 minutes to discover how many minutes are in 1 hour.

Traveling Game: While riding in a car or bus, let each player pick a color. Each car of that color is worth 5 points. The first person to get 50 points wins. Play again, changing the rules so each color is worth 10 points.

The following books include some of the same concepts that are presented in *Leaping Lizards*:

- COUNT ON PABLO by Barbara Derubertis

- THE KING'S COMMISSIONERS by Aileen Friedman

- ARCTIC FIVES ARRIVE by Elinor J. Pinczes